RESTORATION ~~OVER~~ OBLITERATION

Shanequa Watkins

ACKNOWLEDGMENTS

I have to especially thank God for helping me through this piece of my life. I have to extend a special thank you to everyone who helped me stay alive whether that was through direct communication or indirect communication. Thank you for pouring into me and fulling your purpose in my life by being obedient. Had it not been for you, important parts of my healing would have been held up. Last but not least, I have to thank myself for being open to heal. I deserve it and even though the roads taken weren't always he quickest ways; the destination never changed.

CONTENTS

...oh there won't be any

No chapters, no titles, no formalities, or technicalities.

Only the love of writing

The freedom in finally being able to say it

And the healing from releasing it

Welcome to restoration.

Disclaimer

Before you start reading, I'll tell you that this book will not be like your usual book. It won't have chapters or titles. Not only would that have stressed me out, but it also would have made me feel obligated to put a title on every phase I went through while living it. I won't make myself feel like that and I don't think anyone else should either. For those who have titles, then title it but for those who don't; know that it's okay. I hope the reading without labels does not cause you anxiety in any form lol. While reading this, I do pray for you because the content is heavy. I pray that the words minister to you wherever you're at in your life. I pray that your heart, spirit, and mind are open to be changed in this moment. I pray that you understand that God will meet you right where you are and transform you if you allow him to. Lastly, I pray for your freedom from whatever may be holding you in a place of bondage. Thank you for taking this journey with me.

Romans 5:12 NLT "When Adam sinned, sin entered the world."

There I was lying on the cold wood floor in my upstairs master bedroom. The music was blasting so loud that I could feel the beat of it in my heart. The floor was soaked in tears and snot. My home was filled with shadows of unhappiness. I'd got my sister to take my daughter two days before because I was having thoughts of suicide due to my overwhelming feelings of being unwanted and unworthy. I remember sitting up in physical pain because of the intensity of pain I was in emotionally. I've always believed that if your heart is hurting enough that it takes a toll on your physical body. I started whispering God, I'm alone I'm alone I AM ALONE. That whisper turned into a loud yell and then more crying. I picked up my phone hoping that I had a missed call or voicemail from a number that I had blocked. When I didn't, I felt a sense of relief but pain because I didn't feel as important as I once thought I was. I wanted to call but when I fought not doing it, I knew the cycle was starting to end. I know it sounds like it was the ending of something really good but the truth is that it was the ending of the longest, worst relationship I'd ever been in. The ongoing battle between myself and my flesh. It was a battle that I'd fought my entire life, like many people. My flesh or my Earthly wants and desires came at me so hard that I gave up fighting back and decided to let "whatever was going to happen, happen."

Matthew 11:28 NIV "Come to me, all you who are weary and burdened, and I will give you rest."

I thought I had the answer which should have been GET UP, like I often tell other people. My mind said the words YOU CAN DO THIS, but everytime it did; more tears came out. I thought about how many times I'd said that to somebody who was in a place of agony. The words it's okay, you will be okay, the decision you made was the right decision replayed over and over. I thought those words that I so often used brought comfort but saying them had no effect on how I was feeling. How crazy was it that I didn't realize how unhelpful they were until I was saying them to myself? Every word that I tried to mutter to lift myself up did the complete opposite. I sat there in silence thinking that the last few years of my life had determined what the rest of my life would be like and I wanted out. I wanted to be free. I wanted it to be easy. As hard as it is to read the words now, I wanted to die. When the words didn't work, my next thought was to mentally go to a happy place. I started thinking about my daughter because if I ever needed a reason to stay alive, she was it. She was and is the purest and rawest form of joy and love in human form. I thought about who would take care of her if I went through with it and if she would have questions about what happened to me. Then I thought about the custody battle that might take place. Questions raced through my mind, but the final questions were who would I leave my daughter to be and did I really want to miss out on it because I felt like my heart was breaking so bad that it would lead me to my place of death? I understood in that moment that suicide isn't something sudden. It's a well thought out plan or at least in my world, it would have to be because it wasn't just me. Apparently, the plan to end my life wasn't one that only I had. Evil voices swarmed through my mind that hadn't ever festered as much as they did this day. I could hear a voice loud and clear telling me how to end my life. The devil wanted to end me, he wanted me to be selfish. I screamed as my prayers and my thoughts overlapped each other. I closed my eyes and took a deep breath, then I made a choice.

Psalms 139:1 "O Lord, you have examined my heart and know everything about me."

In my moments of pain mixed with rage, I was logical. I knew not to throw or break my phone because I would need it. I knew not to punch holes in the walls because I would have to pay for the damage. I knew not to go out and start a fight with anybody because I would most likely go to jail. I knew not to have sex with a random stranger because it wouldn't heal me. I knew not to do drugs or alcohol because after the high, I would probably end up in a situation that was far worse than the one I was already in. I also knew myself. I knew that I couldn't handle something one time because of my then addictive personality. If I'm being honest, I wanted to do all of it. I wanted to feel a sense of relief no matter what that meant doing to get it. I felt like I deserved to do something reckless because I was hurting. I tossed my phone on the bed and slid back down to the floor. I felt hopeless. I stared at the wall until I had to get up. My older sister had called multiple times to check on me and I knew it would only be so long before she was knocking at my door. I had to make sure that if she did, I was ready. I got up and started to put on the same game face I'd put on most days. I liked to call it "MY LIFE IS GREAT" face. I'd had to wear it for so long because I'd been taught that you never show what you're feeling. You don't look weak because if you did, that's exactly how people would treat you. I sent my sister a text telling her that I was talking to the phone company so she wouldn't be worried. After that, I started my day. Over the last few years,

I'd learned how to hide scars and pain well. I washed my face with an exfoliator and soaked it in cold water. I put my contacts in solution to clean them. I took a hot shower so that my body wasn't tense. I had my lines prepared if it did look like I'd been crying. I would tell my sisters that I'd been doing worship. I'd tell my daughter that my tears were happy tears. I realized in those moments that the truth was so easy to hide, even with a heart and face full of pain. I chose to lie because I was too afraid to let them into that part of my life. I didn't want to let them in because I wasn't ready for healing from what I was dealing with yet. Bigger than that, I wasn't ready to give up what was hurting me.

John 4:10 NLT "If you only knew the gift God has for you and who you are speaking to, you would ask me, and I would give you living water."

After I did my full routine, I stalled around the house until the sun started setting. If I had to pick my daughter up, I wanted to go back home and straight to bed. I knew if I waited late enough, my sister would feed her and make sure she was fully prepared for school the next day. My plan was to play music on our 10-minute ride home to avoid the questions that I knew she would have. Then I would tuck her in so that she didn't have to see me in the place I was in. Thankfully, she's not one of those children who stays up all night. My child loves to get her rest. She is very attentive and semi clingy. She liked to be close to me and right now, I didn't want that. She could look at me and just notice when something was off. Maybe she felt my spirit too. I'm sure that when I was off or when my mental just wasn't where it needed to be; she could sense it. Usually when she does, she stares at me and asks if I'm okay. I didn't have the strength to lie to her or pretend that I was. Yes, I pulled a "responsible" cowardice move. I couldn't be a parent and deal with my pain. As I drove to my sister's house, I decided that I just didn't want to go through the process of trying to hold it together. I told my sister that I had to go back to my office to type last minute notes because my laptop wasn't working. I over stressed that "I'd been typing those notes on my laptop all day and now the laptop had suddenly stopped working." My sister offered to keep her another night so that

I wouldn't have to drive to the other side of town after I'd had such a long day working. Blah blah blah don't act like you've never lied to get a babysitter. All I had to do now was make it through the night to start the next day.

Proverbs 18:24 NLT "There are "friends" who destroy each other, but a real friend sticks closer than a brother."

It was the worst, I mean first day of the week; Monday and I had to go back to work. Knowing that I had to be up early, I stayed up crying half the night. No, I wasn't running off fumes or anger; I was exhausted. I felt like I'd been up drinking all night. My body ached, my eyes were puffy, my nose was stuffy, and my mind was not at half functioning capacity. I had a job telling people what I thought would be in their best interests and how to fix their life when mine was completely upside down. Imagine being forced to show up for others when you can't even show up for myself. I tried to sneak past the 3 offices before mine without being noticed but that never worked when I wanted it to. I knew that I had a million things to do so my plan was to keep conversations simple and short. That plan went south pretty fast when I was called for our 8:30 weekly team huddle. As I sat there listening, I felt intensity run through every bone in my body. The meeting had nothing to do with my personal life but for some reason my emotional being related the topic "how to live a better life to protect vulnerable children." Yeah, I related to that much more than I cared to admit then. My inner self asked how am I protecting my child if I keep putting her through this because of my selfishness? How am I protecting her if I'm not even there for her? How can I create a safe space for her to express herself when all I do is run, hide, and lie instead of facing what I'm feeling? I took off speed walking to my office in tears. People assumed that it was because of my work frustration but it was so much deeper than that. My partner worker rushed to my office and closed the door telling me that whatever it was, it would be okay. It wasn't the first time she'd seen me like this, but this time was by far the worst and certainly the last. She so easily related to the stage of life I was in and was always gentle with her honesty. The cycle I was in was one that had repeated itself quite a bit. She would tell me that it was okay to walk away from people I loved to heal without ever making me feel judged. I turned off all my lights and just melted into my office chair. She walked out to give me space for a few minutes and came back and said "partner let's go, you need to get out of this office for a little bit." I knew that I had to start moving back into reality or I was going to drown, but right now that was so

hard. We left and I listened to her talk. I said
what I could say at minimum to her then
tucked everything into a hypothetical closet
and shut down.

1 Peter 5:7 NLT "Give all your worries and cares to God, for he cares about you."

I knew that once I picked my daughter up, it was game time again. I avoided my sister because I didn't want her to see me like this for the billionth time. I don't remember answering any calls or texts that day. I probably fell into the category of parental neglect a few times. I made sure my daughter was safe, that she wasn't starving or any of that but I was mentally checked out of the real world. The next day came, and the pretending got easier but the crying and thoughts of suicide didn't let up. I started my usual routine. I took my daughter to school and went to work. Work was obviously easier because of my breakdown the day before. I'm not sure if everyone was nervous or honestly worried. I disregarded recommendations to take time off because everyone thought I was experiencing burnout and I wasn't. I knew that I didn't want to go home because I would get lonely and cry. I knew that working would keep me moving and my mind focused on something other than myself. That's when I got the brightest, stupidest idea. Well not the stupidest idea, but a very stupid idea. To hide my problem a little better, I picked up a second job. I left my primary job early and the very first place I saw, I applied at. It was a counseling agency in the same building. What would make me think to pick up a second job or that I was in a space to counsel people? When I had to reflect on it, I could only think of two reasons: selfishness and wanting to try to make things work without God. My primary job was Monday-Friday; my secondary job was every weekend. I threw myself into overdrive because keeping busy was helping me. Me helping myself was a good thing for my daughter. That is the actual lie I told myself. I knew that I wasn't helping anyone and that my attempt to suppress my pain by overworking would catch up with me. You don't have to ask but yes, my family tried to talk me out of it. To keep them off my back, I added the story line of getting out of debt faster; that back up excuse was always somewhere close. We all left it at that because it was clear to them that I was going to make my own decision. They supported my decision and watched it unfold. I was a little over 2 weeks into my second job and my cap blew off. I went in on a Monday during my lunch break at my primary job to sign paperwork and it happened. I snapped on one of the ladies because I felt like she gossiped too much. I was melting down AGAINNNN. I walked out and emailed my letter of resignation. When they asked why I'd quit, I told them that it was a "hostile work environment." That was the end of my overworking phase. It's not funny but I'm laughing saying to myself: yeah I probably needed to get some help ASAP.

Psalms 103:8 "The Lord is compassionate and merciful, slow to get angry and filled with unfailing love."

I knew I needed help, but I couldn't get it. It was as if something was physically holding me down. I knew that getting help would require me to have honest, tough, and intimate conversations. I couldn't do it over the phone; I would have to sit face-to-face with somebody. I also knew that lying would run me in circles. I wouldn't be able to lie because what I was feeling was too hard to hide. If I started to talk about it; all of my emotions would come flying out. I used the excuse "small cities talk" and I didn't want to be found out if you know what I mean. There were so many reasons, but the biggest was fear. Deep down, I was afraid of what people would think if they knew I wasn't who I'd been portraying to be or if they knew what I was going through. I felt like I had to be a superhero. I wanted to be perfect, I wanted to be the person that everyone wanted to be like. I was creating a fake image for people to love and I hated myself for it. It wasn't that I didn't have a support system because I had a full circle. I had a pastor who was straight forward with me about my relationships. She told me the truth no matter how I felt about it. She taught me to rely on God's word over my feelings. She'd say that my feelings would change but God's word would always be true. I ignored every word she said until I saw it for myself. I had and have my mom, who always reminded me of my value and told me to remember who I was. Not who I was in the present moment but to remember who I was in God's eyes. She was quick to acknowledge what I was going through but faster than that, she would make sure that she told me in other words that "I'm the whole loaf." She would lecture and lecture and, my Lord would she lecture. I complained when I didn't understand it but now I know when my emotions are acting up; it's usually because my spirit needs to be fed. My sisters….., there's so much I can say about my sisters. If you know them, I'm sure you understand what I mean. For those of you who don't, I'll give you a small picture of them through my words. My oldest sister always had the words about how I shouldn't allow people to treat me. Over the last few years, she'd talked to me almost every month about not allowing or giving what I didn't want back. She'd also tell me not to put my daughter through the inconsistency of relationships that weren't healthy with anybody. At the end of each conversation, she would remind me that it was my life and that she just wanted me to be happy. I would dread having to tell her that after all of that good advice that I was going back, knowing that it would all happen again. My sister right above me would always call just to see how I was doing. She understood hard breakups. I would talk to her and just cry telling her it was a hard day and then I would go missing. I think she didn't make a big deal about it because she got that I needed space to heal, not constant reminders of the pain. She would tell me that I couldn't stay where I was, but that I had to trust God and get back up. She's always my glue when I'm falling apart and I have to toss in that God purposefully placed her right where she is. It's so crazy that the same sister she is to me, she's that same sister to my other sisters just in a different way. My youngest sister on the other hand lives freely. She lives to enjoy her life, without worrying about what anyone has to say about it. She gives me the fulfillment of living a carefree life when I need to. She isn't just the life of the party, she's the party of my life. I always tell her this, but she is the REALEST person I know. She reasoned with me when I didn't want to do anything. She was quick to tell me don't worry about anything or anybody, just do you. She would let me vent but when she saw I was just going overboard, she would tell me to get my feelings under wraps. Lol, I love her for that. My family levels me out in areas that I repeatedly fall short in and thankfully what I lack, God gifted them with.

John 15:16 NLT "You didn't choose me. I chose you. I appointed you to go and produce lasting fruit."

I can't say that life started to life because it was already doing that, I just became comfortable with everything around me. Time did what time is supposed to do; it moved. People did what they were supposed to do; they lived. Things did what they were supposed to do; they changed. The world didn't rise and set on my heartbreak so I had to find a way to start living again. I figured the best thing to do was go back to the basics. To dig deep and find the "root" of my problem. The basics meant that I had to deal with my past. The basics also meant that I had to become aware that my present was now a compilation of past experiences and assumptions. The process started and I had to double back to deal with what I thought I'd escaped. The further I dug, the more conscious I became to the fact that I wasn't okay. I was easily triggered, I would often have meltdowns, and I carried a bucket of self-guilt. I don't think anything made me more aware than isolation. I would use sick time to sit in the house alone while my daughter was at school and when I did have any off time, I would pretend to work so that I could have more alone time. I had minutes, hours, and days where I gave into what had now turned into full blown depression. The days where I chose not to showed me how serious of a problem I was creating. I was opening the door for more depression to seep in because I made myself feel like I had to face my issues alone. When I tried to stir myself up to talk to my family about it, I was overpowered by the spirits I'd allowed to surround me for so long. I couldn't fight it, I couldn't shake it, and I for sure couldn't overcome it. How do I get out of this was a question I asked God more than I asked him anything else? His answer was always the same; Shanequa, come back.

1 Kings 18:21 "How long will you be divided between two ways of thinking? If the Lord is God, follow Him. But if Baal is God, then follow him."

I now understand that my actions led me to a life where I felt like God wasn't with me. I felt like he was far from me when truthfully, it was me running from him. I know it sounds bad to say, but I was very familiar with treating my relationship with God the way many relationships in my life had been. I would live undeniably going against what I knew was right. I knew if it ever got down to it; God would be there. He was my fall back or my "safe" plan. I used his love and grace as an excuse to live reckless. I guess I didn't factor in that my sin would lead me to a place of

death no matter how much he loved me.
Every decision came with a price and each
time I made the wrong one; I immediately saw
the consequence. I would play pray telling
God that if I could just hear him, I would be
okay. I didn't feel like I needed wisdom or
understanding of what he said because hearing
him made me feel enabled to keep moving. I
would hear what God said loud and clear but I
took what I needed when I needed it. I didn't
care to build a relationship with him and I'm
not saying, overall I didn't ever want a
relationship with God. I'm saying that it was
tough for me to go running back to the same
person whose calls, texts, and wellness visits
I'd ignored for 6 plus months. Out of the
blue, I was calling God to say hey I know I've
been absent. I saw you trying to reach out to
me but I needed a moment oh and if you can,
I really need your help real quick. My flesh

cringed at the thought of going back to God
after how I'd blatantly disrespected him but
there I was and still, he came for me.
Unconsciously, after he gave me the answer I
wanted I sidelined him again. I didn't see how
my relationship with Jesus would help me in
that present moment because I was selfish.
Spending time with Jesus was too much of a
sacrifice for me with "everything" I was going
through. I turned his answer into my own
antidote because I needed a win. I took my
life back into my own hands and started to
ask, what will make me feel more in tune with
myself again? I knew that forgiveness had
worked before. I also knew that just about
every pain I was feeling boiled down to
something I hadn't fully let go of. Forgiveness
would have been my first step but yeahhhh, I
didn't want to do that yet. I hopped to
something that was in the forgiveness

category; guilt. The difference between forgiveness and guilt in my world is that guilt was releasing myself from what I knew I'd done that was ethically or morally wrong. Forgiveness was releasing me from what I'd done or what others had done that was spiritually, physically, or emotionally wrong that had affected any area of my life. I made a list of what I felt guilty about, which was mostly relationships (sexual and friendships). I'd had friends and partners who made horrible decisions but I'd also been on the other end where I was the one who made the horrible decisions. Ehhh, yes contrary to what I would tell myself to sleep at night; I was sometimes the bad guy. That was a hard fact when in my head for years, I'd been the hero who got damaged trying to fix everyone else. I stared at the list so I could work up the nerve to apologize and then fear snuck in. The enemy told me that if I apologized, I would be the weird person in the middle of someone's conversation. I mean, people had continued living their life and out of nowhere I was going to apologize to them. I hadn't ever planned on apologizing because who does that? I mean you cut ties and just leave it at that; nobody cares who was right or wrong. It mattered and deep down, I knew some of my actions had hurt people. Being able to admit when I'd done wrong and going back to fix it wasn't just letting go of guilt, it was renewing my character. In my renewal, I started to find freedom. It required me to take a lot of deep breaths, but I closed a lot of swinging doors by apologizing and having an honest conversation. Please notice that I didn't say I restarted any friendships or relationships because that isn't what God told me to do.

Exodus 20:5 NLT "I lay the sins of the parents upon their children; the entire family is affected."

Can you imagine the high I was on after that first taste of victory? Yeah it felt pretty darned good. Don't get me wrong, I loved every friend I had. I had to learn that everyone not being able to go everywhere with me wasn't a bad thing. It just meant that we were all growing in different places and spaces. My next step was facing all the lies I'd left behind. That was a strechhhhh. I didn't go back to correct every lie because I would have been on a lifetime quest. I did, however, become honest with myself. I'd buried some things because I was ashamed. I also buried some things because I just liked to reminisce for whatever reason. Both of those reasons, but also because sometimes lying was my hiding place. I can literally remember downloading apps to save pictures or messages to have as a cover up if I felt like someone was trying to play me. I would make up lies to have something to say instead of being truthful and setting a boundary. Whew, I had to confront that hurt. Even though I had no intent of doing anything with the memories, something kept me bound to them. I know I'm not the only one but I will tell you that there are only certain memories you should hold on to; that'll be another conversation for another day. The biggest step for me kind of felt like I was joining recovery and since I've now done that; I realize that is exactly what I was doing. I found a person who I won't say that I trusted, but a person I'd been afraid of telling

the truth to. The first opportunity I got, I let

all of my secrets out. I stopped a few times

mid thought thinking OMG, Shanequa did

you really do that? Then there was that other

voice saying, yes honey you did. After 10

minutes of secret talk, I laughed and said

wow, is that what being honest feels like? If

you haven't found that freedom or courage to

be honest with yourself and others, then you

are being deprived of your best life. I say

deprived but that doesn't mean the truth was

easy and it for sure didn't always feel good but

it most definitely held to the reputation of

what I'd always heard which was that the truth

will set you free. I felt a rush of freedom and

you can believe what you want but honesty

for some people makes them feel good. After

I learned to tell the truth, I probably

developed word vomit. Telling the truth didn't

come natural for me before because if you could lie good enough, you could get out of anything. When honesty became a habit, all I wanted to do was share that with people that mattered to me. I opened up to my inner circle about the double D's in my life: depression and divorce. I probably overreacted when I got their response but sometimes I'm like that. I'm not sure how I wanted them to respond because none of their words could have helped me cope. I openly admitted to them that I felt like we didn't talk about things that were real and honest. I sent a long text message then left our group text. That was my way of showing them that "I was drawing a line for what I wanted." Really my attempt to get some attention. I guess when I noticed that I wasn't the only one unable to start a hard conversation, I reflected on the adults in my life. I evaluated how many real conversations I'd had with my parents or any adults I was close to. At most between both parents, it was probably 2 to 3 conversations during childhood that I can remember. The things that were never dealt with had come to torment me. It wasn't just my issues I was dealing with, it was a generational fear of being able to open myself up for honesty. I felt like I kept running into issues which led me to leaving every group I was in until I thought people were ready to talk about what I wanted to talk about. Yeah, I know forced manipulation right? I took a break from the world as a whole, I even left social media. I was still trying to heal on my own. While I was addressing internal issues, I left everything external out. I had given up taking care of myself on basic levels. I'd stopped bathing daily, I wouldn't eat until I had a migraine, I didn't leave the house other than for work or dropping my daughter off, and let's not even mention combing my hair. I had a growing puff that I didn't take care of at all; I would slap a taste of water in it and put on a headband. I have a nonstop love for cleaning but even that was gone. Nothing was working so I referred to a quote I'd heard a long time ago which was "the better you look, the better you feel." That's a full on thing now and since I hadn't ever practiced self-care, I figured it couldn't hurt. I'd read that if you clean your house every day and open your blinds for natural light, it would uplift you. I also read that exercising would help depression go away so that's what I did. I opened my blinds every day and I went outside for at least 20 minutes to walk. In hindsight, I knew that my family would notice how serious my depression was if I kept ignoring everyone so I would ask for their kids every weekend. I won't lie,

absorbing and recharging through their joy
was heaven on Earth. I started cranking my
walks up a little by playing music. Music kind
of starts either an automatic turn up or an
automatic turn down in my head. I would turn
on music that had no meaning, it just made
me want to dance. That added a piece of help
because I was able to relax my mind without
the pressure of trying to figure everything out.
Listening to beats gave my heart some ease.
The twerking music usually kept me upbeat
but after the rush of working out, I wanted to
still feel like I was turning up or coming down.
I started to listen to songs that had more
depth than what made me just want to put my
hands on my knees. I listened to all kinds of
music, most of it wasn't Christian music
because when I play that, I typically need to
be prepared to sit down. I replayed a song I'd
heard at church by a group called Maverick

City called "Man of Your Word." That group led me back to a song by Tasha Cobbs called "This Is a Move." Then there was my song by Hillsong, "Even When It Hurts." Those three songs taught me different lessons. The first song taught me that no matter where I was, God was still a man of his promises. That I might have to deal with the consequences of my choices, but God wouldn't go back on his word because of my weariness. The second song taught me that no matter what life was throwing at me, I always needed to have the ability to welcome the Holy Spirit in to change me. Everything was a move; from one place to the next physically or spiritually. The third song taught me that even when it hurts, which sometimes life will; Jesus is still with me in my pain waiting. On the other end, I listened to SZA, 6LACK, and Wale. SZA had a story that would often take me up and down. I would listen to "Love Galore," which often made me feel like I'd dressed people up in my mind to feel loved. 6LACK, yeahhhhh his music took me to a place of cruising. His song "Pretty little Fears," gave me a different perspective on thinking that people only wanted to know the inner parts of me to hurt me. The song overall talks about being comfortable enough with someone to be able to let your guards down instead of always being afraid. I have a love for almost all of Wale's music but my favorite is "Expectations." It's a song about just trying to fulfill the expectations of people, while trying to figure out who you are. To me, it's also about understanding that you can't pour into people from an empty cup. I know the song refers to a relationship, but it only made me think of Christ. How for years, my goal was to date someone to feel loved but because I was searching for myself in someone else instead of God first; my cup ran dry. Finding the space to be okay with that is okay. I'm a music person so I would rotate it all. I had to let you guys into my musical playlist; you're getting to a glance at everything else.

1 Kings 18:37 NLV "Answer me, O Lord.
Answer me so these people may know that
You, O Lord, are God. Turn their hearts to
You again."

The working out helped me lose weight. The
music gave me a high. The cleaning made me
feel more organized. It all contributed to my
healing until it didn't. Temporary fulfillment
always left me feeling like darkness was
waiting to weigh in on me. I didn't know what
I was supposed to do next so I started
evaluating my family relationships again. I
NEEDED to feel seen, and that was very
often my biggest problem. I also rock a little
too hard in my rocking chair sometimes but I
knew that I'd left a bad taste in a lot of
mouths. I took a step of being the branch that

I wanted and started trying to make some relationships right. I'd started havoc everywhere with my drama so I apologized to my sisters and to the family of the person I'd last ended a relationship with. I didn't apologize because the relationship had ended. I knew that God couldn't use me in their lives unless my heart was right towards them. I didn't just think they had a problem with me, I had a problem with them because I was hurt that they would have to pick a side so I picked mine first. My guard was up. I apologized because for years, I'd not only involved them in toxic situations but I'd made them watch what I knew wasn't good for anybody. My selfishness, whether they admit it or not; changed the trajectory of our relationships. After them, I had to give the hardest apology that I've ever given in real time. I had to apologize to my daughter who had a front row seat to the entire show. She'd seen it from start to finish no matter how much I wanted to keep it from her. After that, I expected things to just go back to how they were before all of it went wrong. I wanted everything microwaved but I had to start rebuilding what I'd taken place in tearing down. It felt good to apologize and fix it instead of pretending the issues would disappear if I didn't talk about them. I felt like I could breathe again but then a harder part came; the process and waiting part. (A LITTLE TIME PASSES, AND I DO MEAN A LITTLE). Okay, that part was hard for me. I wanted my life to change and it wasn't happening fast enough. I wasn't patient with anybody and a bad pattern that I'd learned was that once I apologized, everything should be fixed. WRONG! Apologizing was the first step to me healing, not the people I'd hurt. I tried to rush years of unaddressed issues into a 3-month healing process. I got tired. Tired of living in the same house I'd prayed for. Tired of going the same places. Tired of seeing the same people. Tired of going to the job I'd wanted for almost 4 years. I was just tired. The resolution that I came up with was that I needed a brand new start in a brand new place with brand new people. I had no idea where I wanted to go or what I wanted to do but I knew I wanted to go. One day while I was at work, I started thinking about something I'd always wanted to see…The Grand Canyon. Mind you, I hadn't ever done research to see where the Grand Canyon was but when I did, I found out that it was in Arizona. After that, I started to job hunt and said that prayer that many of us say to ourselves, God if it's what I should do, then give me a sign. A sign for me was getting a job offer. I was denied by 5 jobs. That wasn't enough so I applied for a few more and finally, I got a yes. I ignored the "denied 5 times," and said that was the devil's work. I thought for sure the sign to move was when a job finally said yes. I'd applied at an elementary school, something I had no clue of. After my interview, they said they were willing to hold the job for me until I could find a place. I prayed about it and God told me to stop running. I knew what he meant but I said you're right God. I can't run from an opportunity like this. I talked to my family and pastors about it, everyone said the same answer. They wanted me to hear God. Yes, I knew how I just couldn't right now. I needed someone to give me the answer because my mind was so distorted that I didn't think I would hear the right answer. I knew that leaving meant I would have to drop every commitment I had but staying meant I would have to be unhappy. My selfishness told me that they just didn't want me to leave and that I deserved to see the world. I was high strung on my emotions, so I made an emotional decision.

Isaiah 43:18 NLT "But forget all that—it is nothing compared to what I am going to do."

I gave my job my letter of resignation asked my pastors to release me from church. I did things in some type of decency and order. I'd found an apartment by searching Google and a pretty impressive school for my, things were falling into place. I started looking for moving companies because I really didn't want to re-buy everything, I mean some of the stuff I could do without but not all of it. All the moving companies wanted $8000 or more to move the stuff in my tiny townhouse. It was only a 20-hour drive, they were crazy. I could have packed the stuff into a truck but I knew I wouldn't have anybody to help me unpack it so I looked for professionals. Google only gets you so far if you aren't physically in a place. In other words, that plan didn't work so I moved to the next best thing which was finding a truck that was big enough to pack some stuff in and pull my car. That's exactly what I did. I found a beautiful sparkly white BMW SUV. I thought it was big enough but that wasn't important because it was cute. Y'all my priorities were all out of whack. I was about to be out of a job and before I knew anything about towing a car, I impulsively bought it. Days after, I found out that my SUV wasn't big enough to pull my car and now I had to figure out how to get 2 vehicles across the world. Baby, I was digging a hole quicker than a ground hog. Now I'd forced myself to have only one decision which was to get rid of everything. I got so frustrated with the packing part that I tried to sell my house. Thankfully, my realtor had a list full of things she felt I should do that I wasn't willing to pay for. She then told me if I wasn't willing to do the work to increase the value to what I wanted that I could rent it out. SCOREEEE!!!! I WAS GOING TO BE A LANDLORD. I got a list of management companies and did the bare minimum to rent my place out. My house was already nice, it just had a few holes; I mean dents here and there. The management company did all the handwork as far as listing it and finding a tenant so I carried on. I listed everything in my house on Facebook Marketplace and whatever didn't get sold, I gave away. I found a car shipping company that let me pack some stuff in my car so I stuffed it and dropped it off to my oldest sister until the company was able to haul it. I packed everything else into my other car; two tvs, 3 blankets, a pillow, a few totes full of shoes and clothes, and the cute things my daughter had made over the years. After we emptied the house, we semi moved in with my other sister to enjoy as much time as we could with them before we left. I didn't want to move, I really didn't but I couldn't go back now that I'd done all this. I was highkey terrified. Two days before we set off my sisters gave me the best going away surprise party. It was just what I needed. I don't remember much of it but I know everytime I looked up, I saw somebody I loved. They sat me on a crate in the middle of a park dancing around me and throwing money at me. I sat there and cried like I was a newborn baby who'd just got butt smacked for the first time. It was a sad moment, but in the words of Wayne; if we ain't do nothin else, we was gon ball! My daughter saw me crying and immediately felt the realness of us leaving. I knew I couldn't fix how she was feeling, but

I could help make her feel less alone. I did what any parent in my position would have done, I got another child! My quiet 2-pound bundle of joy, Pup was the most perfect puppy I've ever seen. Oh, did you think I meant a literal child? Heavens no! Pup was tiny, cuddly, sweet, and she gave my daughter an unimaginable sense of relief. We went to church the next morning then took off. I stalled longer than anybody I've ever known, but it was finally time. I cried the entire drive stuffed into my SUV. For those of you wondering how it was for my daughter, it was pretty hard. I gave her pep talks every few hours reminding her that life changes for everybody and that sometimes that change involves moving away. I talked to her about different family members that had moved away or those who had moved back home to discover life for themselves. I feel like it soothed her knowing that she wasn't the only child who moved away from home. I'll know for sure when she's old enough to tell me how she really felt about it. I feel like I have to mention that Texas is the size of the entire United States. I was literally stuck in Texas for 2 days. I high tailed it for 10 hours straight only stopping when I needed to. And then I was forced to stop, not only because I was tired but because I guess my SUV had blown some type of something that I wasn't familiar with. I wasn't going to try to figure out how to fix it, so we stopped at a hotel to rest for a few hours. The next morning, despite the warning signs on my car we finished the drive. AYEEEE, we made it to Arizona! And like the song says, it was day one of the rest of our lives. Yes I like to sing so you gotta get used to that.

Matthew 16:15 NLT "Then he asked them, "But who do you say I am?""

My adrenaline was pumping so fast. The first 10 minutes of driving through Arizona all I saw were dust storm warning signs. Coming from Louisiana, nothing about the weather scares you except the heat. I learned pretty quick that if you can't beat a dust storm, you better pull over. Still, everything was so beautiful. There were mountains and rocks everywhere. I wanted to sight see but I had to make sure my coins were in order. I decided to go to my job before I went anywhere else to do a quick meet and greet. I didn't have the time to sit and go over pay dates and all that good stuff so after about 10 minutes, I left to head to my new apartment. I was walking on clouds taking in all the fresh clean air and new sceneries. When I turned into the complex, I instantly noticed that I got catfished. I drove around the complex scoping it out and saw one of the apartment doors open with supplies sitting in the doorway. It was clear that somebody had just moved out and maintenance was doing repairs. I tried getting permission to look in first but it must have been meant for me to see it without the "extra guided tour." I peeped in and yelled, but nobody answered so I let myself in. After that, I walked around the complex talking to people who lived there. I made my daughter and dog walk with me too so I didn't look like a weirdo questioning people. When I tell you, I ran out of that complex so fast that I left a tire mark I'm not exaggerating. There was no way I was going back there so I called the complex and hypothetically pushed my move in date back. I say that everything is a sign so maybe this one was to give me more time to find the right place. I thought moving into an apartment was an easy process mostly because of how things were back home. I'd never really had to pay anything other than a small deposit if that. All of the places here required a background check, previous rental history, a good credit score, insurance, income that was 3-3.5 times higher than your rent, and actual check stubs. I thought about looking for a person who was renting a place, but after watching tv shows about creepy landlords in big places; I was iffy about that. It was also pretty hard to find an individual instead of a company, I guess everybody was going corporate. I went to about 3 other complexes that day who all said that to even start the process I would have to pay an application fee of $350. I had money saved and I was planning to be making almost $5000 a month, I wasn't worried about them fees. I paid it and was told by each place that because I had no rental history on my credit, I would have to pay a deposit for the same amount as my rent. All of the apartments were $2300 a month or higher. I had money but I was not about to come off all that at one time, so I found a hotel for the night. The next day, I started my truck and it was shaking with thick white smoke fuming out. That truck was not about to slow me down so I drove it anyway. The hotel we'd stayed at was 40 minutes away from my job but I knew I had to show my face and do my paperwork. They had me sign everything, do a grand tour, meet everybody, and then gave me my keys. Now I know I should have thoroughly read and asked questions before I signed my contract in person but I didn't. I signed all of it before I asked for specifics about my exact pay and details. I just knew I was about to be making bank and assumed that my pay would be my pay no matter when I started. I know you can tell where this is going, SO YES it was my first contract job. I found out later that day that my pay was aligned with my start date which had changed when I didn't start on the date that my contract started. Okay, don't piece stuff together quicker than I did because I have my moments where it takes me a while to catch on. My overall salary now was decreasing by $10,000. If you do the math, that was about $500 less per check or $1000 a month! It doesn't sound like a lot but in the words of one of my favorite movies, "Frankie I NEEDED THAT MONEY!" I didn't let that shake me much because what was I going to do? I couldn't drive back in my smoking truck and I couldn't quit my job without having a backup plan. I had to suck it up and figure it out. I did that, I didn't get extra sassy or none of that, I just went on. The day was stomping a mud hole in my tail. Let me add the icing to the cake for you, the school I'd initially applied for my daughter to attend was now 30 minutes away from our hotel. I was willing to take that drive for a little while but then they mentioned a small detail that maybe I didn't pay attention before, they were closed on Fridays. They didn't offer any type of alternative programs so I had to look for daycares. The daycares in Arizona were outrageous, they all wanted at minimum $100 a week or $40 for 1 drop in day. Yeah, I wasn't doing that. Here I was across the world with a fresh car note on a truck that was shaking and blowing smoke, a job that dropped my pay, nowhere to live, and now no

school for my daughter to attend. Things
weren't falling apart, they had FALLEN.

Matthew 7:11 NLT "So if you sinful people know how to give good gifts to your children, how much more will your heavenly Father give good gifts to those who ask him."

All of my frustration and disappointment led to a phone call with one of my sisters who told me to just stop, pray, then plan. She told me that she knew I hadn't heard God to move and think he wouldn't work things out for me. Bigger than her words, she helped me to logically think of a plan. After I calmed down, she told me to just stay at the hotel until I found a different place. Then she told me to look for resources by calling the salvation army, or any places that helped homeless people. She gave me the idea to drive around in different directions to find somewhere else that I wanted to live. Even though I didn't do that; it was a pretty smart idea. None of this was stuff that I didn't know, but I've learned that information doesn't really set in if you don't address the immediate threats first. She asked me when my other car would be delivered. I'd completely forgot that I had another car, that's how discombobulated I was. I called the driver and asked him if we could meet at the dealership instead of him dropping the car off to me at a hotel. When he said yes, small victory and another problem solved. Yes, I'm singing as I type this because the devil thought he would have one up one me. This was one of those "two are better than one" realization moments. Man, God is so good. After I was through all of that, she told me to call my job and tell them what was going on. My ego didn't want to do that because I didn't know these people well enough for them to see me having a vulnerable moment but I did it. It wasn't much they could change; I mean they had already cut my pay. What's the worst they could do to me now? I still had an attitude about my pay but I disciplined myself to do what my sister said because she was right and I knew I couldn't afford to lose my job. The day I picked up my second car I drove around near our hotel, really because I didn't want to go back. I passed by a shopping mall up the street and made one wrong turn trying to get there. That wrong turn led me to my first waterfall view that sat directly in front of an apartment complex. Yesss, I stopped for a selfie and then I decided to try my chances applying at the apartment. I talked to the receptionist about nearby schools and she printed me a full list. The leasing agent told me I would hear back from them in 2-3 days.

While I waited, I went to two of the schools and completed applications. Both schools were open EVERY DAY, I learned my lesson the first time. One school called back and told me that my address was listed as a hotel. She said that living at a hotel pretty much put us in the system as homeless. I was speechless and embarrassed on the other end of the phone. She proceeded to tell me that since I was homeless; my daughter would receive free transportation anywhere within a 30-mile radius, free lunch, Christmas gifts, clothing, gift cards for food, and a discount to the school's after school program if we needed it. I cried all over the place. Jesus literally walked right up on me like there ain't a place you'll ever be that I won't come for you in. My daughter was finally able to start school and everything that I needed came with it, not because of the school but because of GOD!

Two days later, the apartment complex called and denied me because of my income. I went off on the lady a little, but going off wasn't fixing my problem. She told me that my income needed to be almost $1000 more a month, just what I'd been cut at my job. I told the lady that I was renting my house back home and that I had a tenant who paid rent monthly, LYING. She told me that if I had proof, I had 3 days to submit it and I could move in. I left that office in faith praying that my lie manifested into the truth. It didn't happen and I almost started to doubt again that the plan would work but instead, I kept believing for what I needed to happen. The next day, the management company found someone who wanted to rent my house for $100 less a month than what they were asking. I agreed and got a signed lease emailed to me as proof and pudding! I had to pay a few extra fees but WE WERE GETTING INTO AN APARTMENT!

Isaiah 53:5 NLV "But He was hurt for our wrong-doing. He was crushed for our sins. He was punished so we would have peace. He was beaten so we would be healed."

Me and my daughter turned up that weekend like it was nobody's business. We ate out ANDDD ordered dessert! We started our move and waved the hotel GOODBYE! Walking everything up a flight of stairs, we had so little stuff that it took us about 4 hours to get everything unpacked. Quick and easy. I grew up real old school so a pallet to me was just like a mattress. If you're tired enough, you'll fall asleep. My daughter didn't complain any, she was perfectly fine with sleeping wherever as long as I was there. She fell asleep and I melted into the carpet face first. I asked

God to wrap his arms around me so that I
could feel his presence tighter than a blanket.
That melting experience changed my life. I
woke up in the middle of the night just crying
and praying because even though I had to
relearn it, I begin to understand that my
relationship with God wasn't one where he
always had to lecture me, he was often just
there to comfort me. He wasn't there pointing
his finger at me saying I told you so. He didn't
throw in my face that I was where I was
because I chose not to listen. He met me right
where I was and stayed with me. That
realization when I felt like I had nothing else
was my aha moment. Piece by piece, I allowed
God to start putting my life back together.
Being put back together didn't mean he threw
glue on top of my life. I had to allow what was
my life to be totally torn apart. As hard as I
thought it would be, when I eliminated every

other distraction, it was easy to pursue God more. Don't get me wrong, the other problems were still there but my way of fixing them never worked. I came to terms and peace with things working out God's way and in his timing instead of my own. Obviously, the biggest issues were my money and my truck. I was over my monthly budget by $1200. The dealership had called me back and wanted $6000 to fix my truck. I couldn't magically make my problems disappear, there was nothing I could do about them other than wait. I was powerless on my own. I shifted my focus to my present issues, something smaller that I could deal with right then. Furniture and house shopping. Say what y'all want but I needed furniture and retail therapy. On the days when we had spare time, we bargain shopped in all of the nearby cities. Yes, for a good deal, I was willing to drive all the way to the other side of wherever. Our first must have was a couch because we could sleep and watch tv on it. I used one of my trusted credit cards and found a sectional for $1100. That was cheap compared to what I usually spent on furniture. I found a guy to mount my tvs for $75 each and BOOM, my living room was put together and beautiful. It became our game room, our church, and our bedroom for at least 2 months. The other rooms came together slowly with minimal things. I mean minimal like I fully furnished the rest of my house including the kitchen for under $1000. We hadn't found a church yet so every morning we would turn on praise and worship music while we got dressed. After work and school, we got into the habit of sitting down for at least twenty minutes to journal about our day and read it to each other. Instead of trying to hide my bad moments or how I let

God into them, I let my daughter watch my experience. I had to remember that she'd moved too and was probably feeling some of what I felt in different ways. Communication, even though it started through journaling helped me to be a better daughter and parent. I was so thankful for everything, but more than any of the things; I was thankful that I'd learned how to create a safe space for my daughter to honestly talk to me.

Psalms 68:6 NLT "God places the lonely in families; he sets the prisoners free and gives them joy."

Finally, life was starting to become normal. I bargained with the dealership against their recommendations to purchase one of my own parts which saved me $600! I also got approved for a loan through the dealership that covered everything except $1000. I started making a monthly budget plan with a strict accountability partner, my sister. She made me send her pictures of my actual checks and make a list of everything I had to pay monthly. She taught me how to gather my mess and organize it so that I could deal with it. Slowly that organization started to create a real plan for me to work towards maintaining everything I had. What started at $1200 over what I could afford started to change. Renting my place out had brought me down to only being $900 over my budget. Then the unexpected banger was that my child support became steady hahahaha. Yes, I said child support because everything counted. I used credit cards to cover whatever I didn't have and then 2 months later, my financial advisor made me use my little tax check to pay 2 of my monthly bills for 6 months each. I hated her plan but not having to worry about where the money would come from for something I needed was worth wanting to blow my tax money. I would be under exaggerating if I said that God only showed up in bits and pieces of my life. He showed up everywhere. I'd been sideline praying for a physical reminder of home, really a sign of family. I'd tried making small conversation with people to develop friendships but I didn't have anything in common with anybody anywhere we went. After I tried a few times, I stopped because maybe I didn't need friends yet. I found solitude in my confinement. One day in Walmart, I met my sister. A lady walked up to me complimenting my hair and we immediately connected. Her first invite to me was to church, just what I'd been looking for. I knew that she wasn't a coincidence; she was my prayer being answered. She led me to the church that we found home in. She was a single parent with one daughter and somewhat new to Arizona too. I prayed for one person and God sent two so that he could remind me that he cared about my entire being which included my daughter. I had to get to a place of knowing and trusting that God would do it because he did. He always did. The rest of life in Arizona is still being written which means that as it progresses; you guys will have to keep reading.

With nothing but love, Shanequa.